A Parent's Guide to the Junior Cycle

A COLLABORATION BETWEEN

KINSALE COMMUNITY SCHOOL AND THE EXAMCRAFT GROUP

The **Examcraft** Group

Published by

The Super Generation

89F Lagan Road, Dublin Industrial Estate, Glasnevin, Dublin 11

© 2020 The Super Generation

ISBN: 978-1-907330-28-5

Introduction

Transitions in life are never easy and the move from primary to post-primary school can be a daunting prospect for both parents and students.

As a parent, there are many ways you can support your child through this change. This book will give you a better sense of what to expect over the coming months and years, and will provide you with insights into how you can support the different stages of your child's learning journey.

This book is designed to guide you through the structure, format and requirements of the Junior Cycle programme, and to give you an understanding of the thinking behind the programme and the learning experience that your child will enjoy in secondary school.

Along with this, you will get some direction on how you can support your child; initially, through their transition into secondary school, and then through the different stages of their learning journey in post-primary school.

Supporting your child during their first weeks in secondary school

Starting secondary school can be both a little scary and an amazing adventure for young people: new subjects, different teachers, lockers, new sports, clubs, and, best of all, making new friends. However, every young person reacts differently to these new experiences, and it is probably fair to say that every student at some stage during their school life gets worried about school. Especially at the start, young people may feel anxious about:

» New teachers, hard subjects, homework, lockers or relationships

» Coping with difficult social situations, such as making new friends, building confidence, group work or fitting into a larger, more diverse school

» Social media sites

» What other students might think of them

» Lots of other things, as every young person is different.

Young people can start to think about the worst possible scenario in these situations and become anxious about how they are going to deal with them. It's important to help young people navigate their way through these situations so that they feel able to manage these challenges.

Easing the transition to secondary school

Schools are very aware that starting secondary can be a stressful time for many young people, and they have supports and programmes in place to help students during this time. These supports can be divided into two types: *formal* and *informal* school support structures.

FORMAL SCHOOL SUPPORT STRUCTURES

All schools have an induction team in place to support students as they enter secondary school. Normally, this is made up of:

» **A class teacher, sometimes called a class tutor or form teacher, who has specific responsibility for one class group, and**

» **A year head – a teacher who has specific responsibility for the year group.**

Generally speaking, the form teacher/tutor or year head will coordinate the transition activities. These activities usually happen over the first few days of school and are designed to put the children at ease, increase their familiarity with the school, and build relationships.

There may also be one or more teachers with specific responsibility for pastoral support. It may be worthwhile finding out the structures within your child's school to support them in transition, and in talking to your child about the supports available to them.

As a general rule, if a student has a particular challenge, they should normally talk to their class teacher, year head or counsellor for support and guidance.

INFORMAL SCHOOL SUPPORT STRUCTURES

Often as part of the transition support system, a senior student will help first year students. Some of the programmes that schools run include:

» **The buddy system**

» **Big Sister, Big Brother**

» **Guardian Angel**

These are usually year-long programmes with a focus on helping first years during the early months when issues arise, like reading the timetable, finding and using lockers, finding the right room, etc. Senior students can also pass on any worries a student might have to the class teacher, year head, guidance counsellor or chaplain.

Sometimes a new student might just feel a little lonely, and a 'hello' or show of interest from an older student can mean a lot, especially since they look up to them.

The senior students in these leadership roles work to:

» Build a sense of community and belonging in the first year classes

» Plan activities to help young students interact and get to know each other

» Organise activities for other year groups, such as excursions

» Organise non-uniform days

» Organise table quizzes, cinema days, end-of-year sports days, etc.

The activities vary from school to school, but the overall objective is the same – to make the transition to secondary school easier for the student.

What can you do as a parent?

As a parent, you also play a key role in supporting your child in this transition. You know your own child better than anyone else, and are more aware of their feelings.

There are some simple things that you can do to help your child at this time, such as:

» Talking to them and understanding their concerns

» Helping them get organised - for example, making sure they have all the books and equipment they need for each subject

» Helping them to understand their timetable and plan for the day ahead

» Supporting them with their homework

» Taking an interest in their school life, school projects, friends, etc.

Every child is different: some take going to secondary school in their stride, others find it more challenging. But this is the case in every walk of life – we all have different talents and abilities, even as adults. By talking to your child, you'll get a better understanding of how they feel about the transition.

If your child is stressed about their new school, advise them to:

BE POSITIVE

Especially on the first day, focus your questions on what they enjoyed, what they liked most about their new school, and help them to see this as a positive change in their life - something they are well able for.

BE PATIENT

Let them know it's normal for it to take a while to become familiar with a new environment. Encourage your child to give it time and tell them or let them know that it will get easier.

BE ORGANISED

Advise them to get together all the books, copies and equipment that they need; being organised makes the day a lot less stressful.

BE FRIENDLY

Encourage them to talk to their classmates, to introduce themselves, and to be friendly and smile. Once they establish friendships, they will begin to feel part of the school.

Big School: not just big in name!

Some secondary schools can be very big and, especially for students coming from small primary schools, just getting around the school can be daunting for the first few days. For bigger schools, it's common for a map of the school to be given to incoming first years.

If you think your child may have a problem getting around the school, ask them to show you their map, and then ask them some simple questions. You can vary the way you ask the questions so it sounds less like a test! For example:

» Can you show me where you store your books in your locker?

» Can you find the maths class on the map?

» Wow, it's a big building! How do you get from your classroom to the yard?

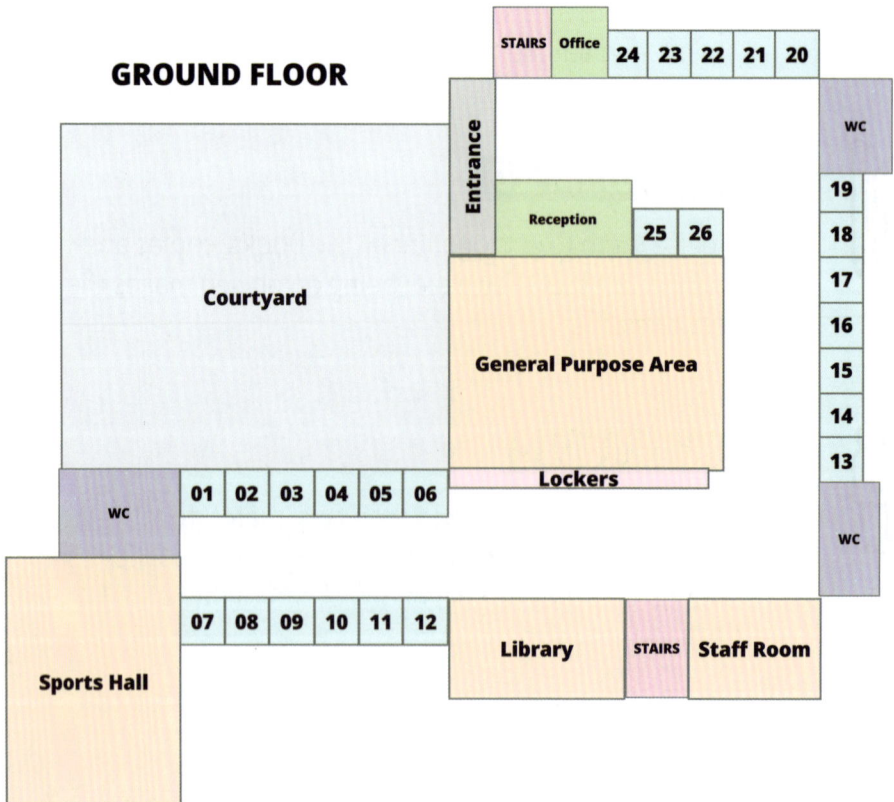

GROUND FLOOR

| STAIRS | Office | 24 | 23 | 22 | 21 | 20 |

WC

Entrance

Reception

25 | 26

19

18

Courtyard

17

16

General Purpose Area

15

14

13

WC | 01 | 02 | 03 | 04 | 05 | 06

Lockers

WC

07 | 08 | 09 | 10 | 11 | 12

Library | STAIRS | Staff Room

Sports Hall

By asking these questions, you can direct your child, while at the same time, they'll be developing their map reading skills. You want to be the 'guide on the side' – so, where possible, you should try to help your child find the right answer, without them becoming dependent on you.

The timetable

One of the biggest challenges for many young people going into secondary school can be the constant change in the day-to-day routine. In primary school, pupils have one teacher all day, usually in just one classroom. In secondary school, however, that routine changes dramatically.

There is a subject change every 40-60 minutes, and with it, a change of teacher - and possibly even classroom. This is recorded on the school timetable, and your child will get a timetable outlining their schedule for the school week.

Time Am	Monday Dé Luain	Tuesday Dé Máirt	Wednesday Dé Céadaoin	Thursday Déardaoin	Friday Dé hAoine
8.50	TUTORIAL R12 Ms. O'Connor	TUTORIAL R12 Ms. O'Connor	TUTORIAL R12 Ms. O'Connor	TUTORIAL R12 Ms. O'Connor	TUTORIAL R12 Ms. O'Connor
9.00	Irish R4 Ms. Ryan	French R9 Ms. Cotter	Irish R4 Ms. Ryan	Geography R13 Mr. Burns	PE GYM Ms. Ryan
9.40	Irish R4 Ms. Ryan	Maths R4 Mr. Porebski	English R6 Ms. Burke	Home Ec. R25 Mr. Fahey	PE GYM Ms. Ryan
10.20	Maths R20 Mr. Porebski	English R20 Mr. Burke	English R6 Ms. Burke	Home Ec. R25 Mr. Fahey	Maths R20 Mr. Porebski
11.00	Break	Break	Break	Break	Break
11.20	German R1 Mr. Fischer	PE GYM Ms. Ryan	Geography R13 Mr. Burns	Irish R4 Ms. Ryan	Business R11 Mr. Abara
11.40	German R1 Mr. Fischer	PE GYM Ms. Ryan	Geography R13 Mr. Burns	Irish R4 Ms. Ryan	Business R11 Mr. Abara
12.20	LUNCH	LUNCH	LUNCH	LUNCH	LUNCH
1.20	Art R25 Mr. Fahey	Home Ec. R25 Mr. Fahey	German R1 Mr. Fischer	Art R25 Mr. Fahey	French R9 Ms. Cotter
2.00	Art R25 Mr. Fahey	Home Ec. R25 Mr. Fahey	German R1 Mr. Fischer	German R25 Mr. Fahey	French R9 Ms. Cotter
2.40	English R6 Ms. Burke	Business R11 Mr. Abara	Maths R20 Mr. Porebski	English R6 Ms. Burke	Art R25 Mr. Fahey
3.20	English R6 Ms. Burke	Business R11 Mr. Abara	Maths R20 Mr. Porebski	English R6 Ms. Burke	Art R25 Mr. Fahey

The timetable is one of the first pieces of information your child will be given on their first day. It's important because it not only tells them their daily lesson plan, but it lets them know about the equipment they will need to get ready the night before. It also tells them the start and finish time of each lesson, in which room it will take place, and which teacher they will have for each subject. They will probably have 6 to 9 different subjects every day, and some will be in special rooms; for example, Science will usually take place in a lab and PE in the PE hall.

Another big adjustment in first year is the number of subjects your child will be studying. In some schools, first years study 12 to 15 different subjects, as they run taster programmes in a range of subjects. This allows the students to decide on their subject based on their personal experience of it.

As a parent, you should try to ensure that your child understands how to read their timetable. You could sit down with them after their first day and ask them some questions:

> » Who is teaching you Maths?

> » In what room does Maths take place?

> » How many periods of PE do you have a week?

Most young people will have no problem with the timetable, as it will be explained in school. However, if they have difficulty understanding it, it can cause a lot of stress. If your child is struggling, you will want to support and reassure them from the start.

TIMETABLE TIPS:

» Students don't have to remember their timetables by heart; they just need to know how to read them.

» Ask your child to write their timetable into their homework journal and make a copy for their study/bedroom.

» If they have a locker in school, a copy should be placed inside the door of the locker.

» Remind your child to check their timetable at night for the next day's lessons. They will then normally look at their timetable at the end of each class period.

» Colour-code the subjects on the timetable to make it instantly clear what subjects they have on what days.

Subjects and teachers

From the timetable, students should be able to complete a table like the one shown below. If you feel your child has difficulty understanding the timetable, you could ask them to complete this.

Subject		Teacher Name	Room
Code	Name		

What do they need for each subject?

It's useful for your child to have a list of everything they need for each subject: it ensures that they don't forget anything when preparing their bag the night before. One of the keys to being organised is for students to develop a system that helps them remember things. Below, your child could record everything they need for their different subjects.

English	Irish	Maths	

P.E.	Science		

Getting organised – simple first steps

To help them to get organised, students should:

- » Put their name on every book and copy

- » Cover their books and copies to protect them from wear and tear

- » Put their name on their uniform and PE uniform

- » Get into the habit of recording their homework in their homework journal, marking off the homework as they complete it

- » Fill in their homework journal every day.

Getting organised for learning

As there are lots of different subjects in secondary school, it's important that students organise their copies and books; having a system for this saves time. Many find the following system useful.

Colour-coding

Colour-code books, copies, etc. That way, when it's time for English, they can just grab all the books with a yellow sticker, or blue for maths etc. They should also colour-code their timetable, using the same colours.

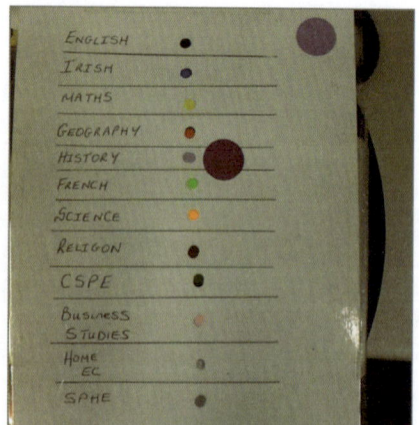

Heavy-duty folders

These heavy-duty folders, sometimes called mesh storage wallets, come in various sizes and are great for holding all the materials they need for each subject in one place.

They are very useful for subjects like technical graphics, art, etc., as all the equipment relating to that subject is stored in one place. While they cost a few euro, they will save you money in the long run, and can often reduce a child's stress as they will spend less time looking for materials.

The school locker, and organising it for learning

In most secondary schools, students are assigned a locker to store their books and equipment.

They will be responsible for this locker and should ensure that it is securely locked at all times.

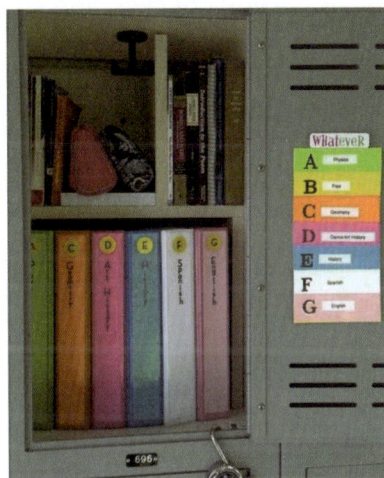

Developing a nightly routine

It's important that from the very start a good, easy-to-follow routine is established at home for what is supposed to happen each evening. All too often, things get pushed to late in the evening, and are either forgotten or ignored. For the first few weeks, until your child gets into the habit of doing it for themselves, you should encourage them to check the following each night:

» Check their timetable to ensure they have the correct books and equipment packed for the following day.

» Do they have their full uniform (tie, shoes, jacket, etc.)?

» Do they have any special equipment they need for tomorrow's subjects (PE gear, ingredients, art materials, etc.)?

» Have they completed all homework for the following day's classes?

» Have you checked and signed their journal?

» Is their schoolbag packed?

» Do they have their locker key and swipe card, if required?

TIPS FOR PARENTS

You can support your child in their early days in secondary school by:

» Making sure they eat breakfast

» Allowing plenty of time for them to get school

» Checking each evening for letters home - such as permission slips, school planners or homework journals to sign - to avoid early morning panic or forgotten items

» Having a spare locker key in an envelope in their school bag and one at home

Homework

Have you heard of the forgetting curve? It shows how information is forgotten over time unless you make a conscious effort to remember it.

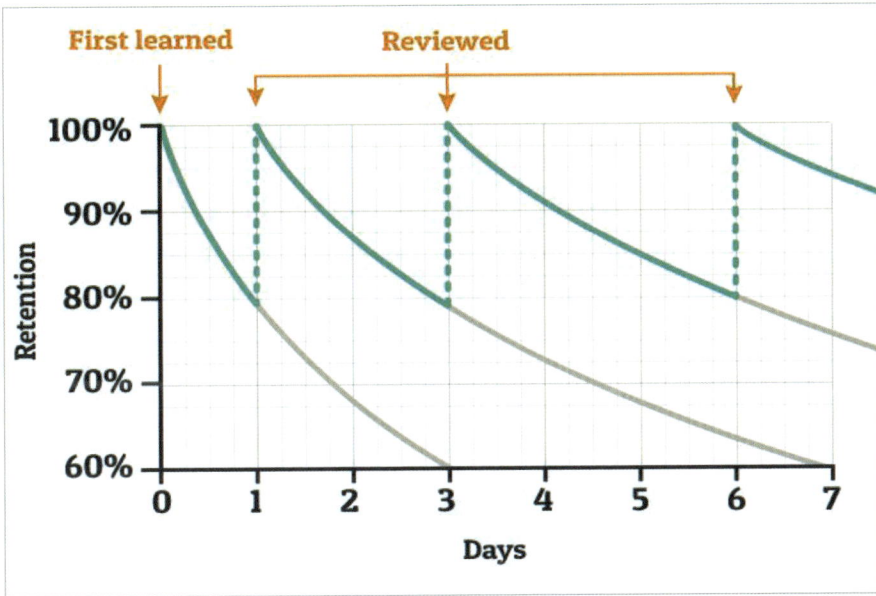

It's important for you and your child to know that it's normal to forget information. It can be frustrating for young people when they understand something in class, but when they come home they have forgotten it, or no longer understand it. However, it happens to everyone, and it explains why homework is such an important part of the learning process.

Homework helps to embed learning, to 'make it stick'. It makes the memory stronger and it acts as the first review. So, homework is vital for success in school, and it is generally based on work covered in class.

To ensure students are clear about what's needed for their homework, schools normally give them a homework journal, where they write down daily the homework given and when it must be completed by. In some schools, parents are required to sign the homework journal on a nightly or weekly basis, which shows that you are aware of your child's homework, and have checked that it was being done.

HOMEWORK TIPS FOR LEARNERS

» When a teacher assigns homework, check when it must be completed by and write it into your homework journal.

» Prioritise homework that must be done for the next day. This allows you time for homework which is due on a later date.

» When you complete your homework, tick that you have completed it, so you can concentrate on what to do next!

HOMEWORK TIPS FOR PARENTS

» The later your child starts, the longer it will take – no first year should be doing homework after 8pm.

» There should be a gap between finishing homework and bedtime. It's good for the young person to switch off and unwind.

» Try to ensure that weekend homework doesn't drift into Sunday. Maybe allow Friday as a homework-free evening as a treat, but homework should then be done on Saturday morning.

» The agreed schedule for homework should be stuck to the fridge with a magnet, like all those other 'forget-me-nots'. In this way, everyone is clear about when homework starts and, just as importantly, when it stops!

		DUE	DONE
orget:			
Gaeilge	Design a poster for a Gaeltacht College describing their Summer Course.	THURSDAY	✓
English	Research your favourite music group – Albums – Songs Achievements	FRIDAY	
Maths	Algebra Qs p.20 a) – d)	THURSDAY	✓
rget:			

As a parent, try to provide the encouragement and environment to support your child - a role that is far more important than you might think. You provide the space, materials, and the food, but you can also have a far more active role without interfering.

Simple questions like *'What have you to do for Irish tonight?'* or *'What did the teacher say about your essay?'* might not get much response, but at least your child will know that you care enough to ask!

Young people who complete their homework as required normally have a structure around homework, i.e. it is done at an agreed time and there is an agreed place to do it. You can help your child by having conversations about creating that structure and routine.

Dinner might be at 6pm, piano lessons on Tuesday at 5pm, football on Saturday at noon, but where is the official slot for homework? Homework is fitted into the gaps between everything else, like filler in a crack! This means that the attention given to the task is broken and lacks purpose.

As a parent, if you can help your child in creating a structure and sense of organisation around homework in the early stages of secondary school, you will be giving them a great gift – one that will stand to them throughout school and into third level and beyond. Learning how to successfully manage time is an invaluable life skill and will make the transition into secondary school a lot easier.

If you create this structure and allocate a time and a place for homework in your house, it will no longer be a dark cloud over evenings and weekends.

Some schools offer supervised study for an hour or two after school. Many students like the discipline of this, as they can then leave school without any further work to do. This can relieve much of the stress around night-time homework.

Helping your child to create structure

Decide with your child on the time when homework is to be done. The time might be different each day, but it needs to be kept to just as much as the time given to a music lesson or GAA training session.

Weekly Study Timetable

TIME	MON	TUE	WED	THU	FRI	SAT	SUN
6am-7am							
7am-8am							
8am-9am							
9am-10am							
10am-11am							
11am-12pm							
12pm-1pm							
1pm-2pm							
2pm-3pm							
3pm-4pm							
4pm-5pm							
5pm-6pm							
6pm-7pm							
7pm-8pm							
8pm-9pm							
9pm-10pm							

Typically, first years spend 1½ - 2 hours per day, although the type of homework may be very different. Certain subjects like Maths, English and Irish get homework every night, others every other day, others weekly.

Of course, it needs to be appreciated that the time it takes to finish homework very much depends on the child. If you believe that homework is causing particular stress for your child, or that they are spending hours at it each night, you should talk to their year head or tutor.

Junior Cycle - new forms of learning

During the Junior Cycle, it's important to be aware that your child will be doing different types of activities for homework, e.g. more active research, presentations, group work, or IT. Support this self-directed and independent learning – engaging in many different forms of learning experience is all part of the Junior Cycle.

Creating a study environment

In an ideal world, all children would have their own desks in their own rooms. But it's not an ideal world, and space varies from home to home.

The kitchen table isn't ideal, as it has to be cleared for meals, and this interruption is exactly what we're trying to avoid. If possible, a separate table in a quiet area could be allocated for homework, where children can keep their materials.

Creative DIY skills can turn a bay window or under-stairs area into a cosy and private space that will be associated with homework alone.

We all know how territorial kids can be, so if we allow them to have this private space, the payback may be higher. A lamp over the desk will give a focal point to the study area, and give a little atmosphere, as well as the necessary light to work efficiently.

The Junior Cycle and Your Child

The Junior Cycle and Your Child

We've looked at how you can support your child during their move into secondary school; now, let's take a closer look at what they'll be learning and what they should expect from the Junior Cycle.

One of the main differences between the old Junior Certificate programme and the new Junior Cycle programme is that now students are at the centre of the learning process. They have a broader range of learning experiences, and there's an emphasis on developing a wider range of skills.

In terms of assessment, where once there was one major final exam in a subject, students are now assessed in several different ways throughout the Junior Cycle, with a final state exam at the end.

The old Junior Certificate has been replaced by the Junior Cycle Profile of Achievement (JCPA). This profile reports on the progress of your child across a range of skills and experiences, which we'll cover later in this book.

The Framework for the Junior Cycle

All curriculum and education programmes in Ireland are set out by the National Council for Curriculum and Assessment (www.ncca.ie). This is done in consultation with stakeholders: parents' organisations, teachers' organisations, trade unions, and other educational interests.

In 2015, the NCCA published the Framework for Junior Cycle, which outlines the various elements of the Junior Cycle. The Framework includes the following elements:

- » **The Eight Principles of the Junior Cycle**

- » **24 Statements of Learning**

- » **The Eight Key Skills**

- » **Subjects, short courses and other learning experiences**

- » **Assessment and reporting**

Below, we go through each of the elements of the Junior Cycle as set out in the NCCA Framework. It's important to remember that schools do have some flexibility in how they deliver the Junior Cycle – they use this framework as a reference to guide their planning process. It can also help you as a parent to understand the rationale and logic behind the programme, and to understand the different elements of the programme.

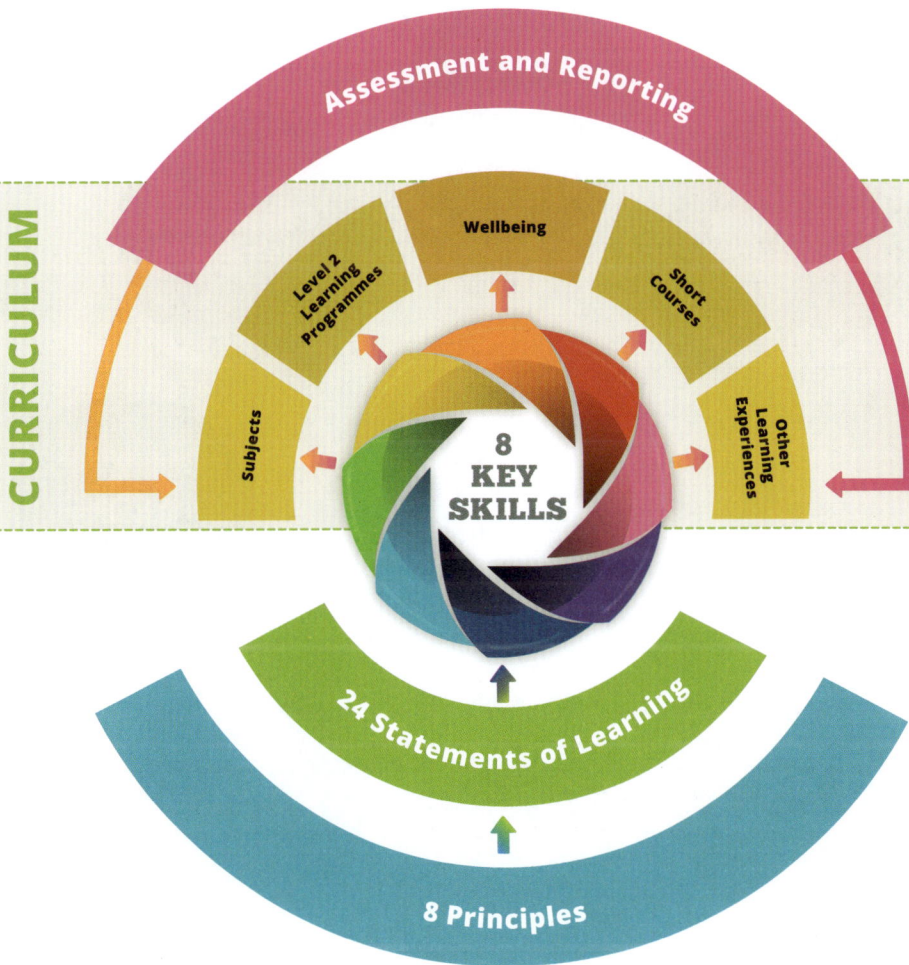

CURRICULUM

Assessment and Reporting

Wellbeing

Level 2 Learning Programmes

Short Courses

Subjects

Other Learning Experiences

8 KEY SKILLS

24 Statements of Learning

8 Principles

The Eight Principles of the Junior Cycle

The Eight Principles of the Junior Cycle are like the 'DNA' of the Junior Cycle programme and are always in the minds of teachers when planning a programme for their school. **The Eight Principles are:**

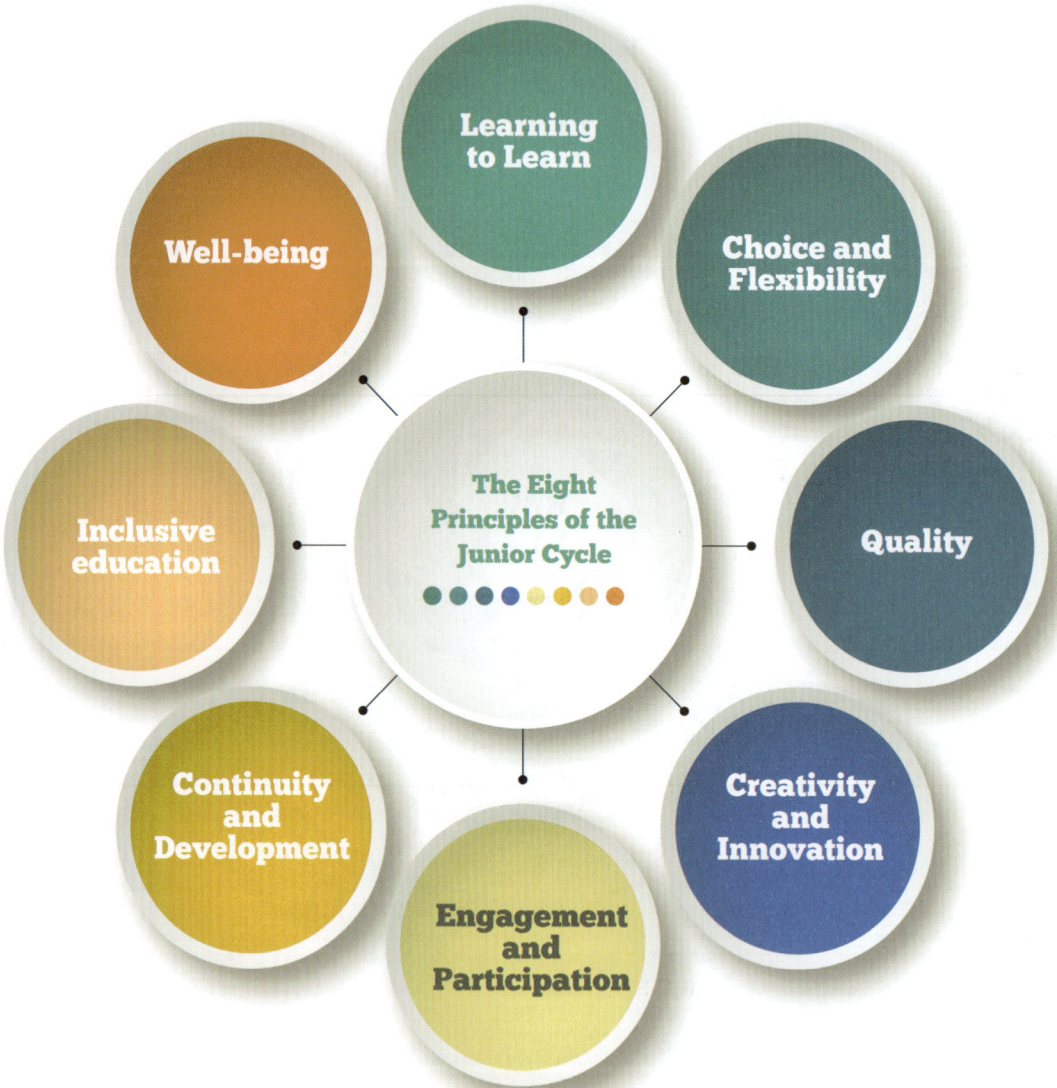

Learning to Learn

Choice and Flexibility

Well-being

The Eight Principles of the Junior Cycle

Quality

Inclusive education

Continuity and Development

Creativity and Innovation

Engagement and Participation

LEARNING TO LEARN

Planning a programme of learning for students to help them develop greater independence in learning to meet the challenges of life beyond school, whether this is further education or working life.

CHOICE AND FLEXIBILITY

The Junior Cycle programme should offer a wide range of learning experiences to all.

QUALITY

Students will have a high quality of education, and high standards will be expected from them.

CREATIVITY AND INNOVATION

Students should be given opportunities to be creative and innovative.

ENGAGEMENT AND PARTICIPATION

The Junior Cycle programme should encourage engagement and enthusiasm in students, and connect with life outside the school.

CONTINUITY AND DEVELOPMENT

The programme should support and recognise students' progress in learning and support their future learning.

INCLUSIVE EDUCATION

The programme should be inclusive of all students, and there should be equality of opportunity, participation and outcomes for all.

WELL-BEING

The Junior Cycle programme should contribute to students' physical, mental, emotional and social well-being and resilience. Learning takes place in a climate focused on the collective well-being of school, community and society.

As a parent, it's a good idea to reflect on these principles. Although they seem quite generic, they do help to draw up a programme of study that will help young people leave the Junior Cycle well prepared for the challenges of the Senior Cycle and the uncertainty of the world beyond school.

Statements of Learning

As well as the Eight Principles, the Junior Cycle Framework has 24 Statements of Learning – these are statements of what young people are expected to achieve by the end of the Junior Cycle programme. These are that the student:

1. Communicates well using a variety of means in a range of contexts in the language of the school, i.e. Irish or English.

2. Listens, speaks, reads and writes in their second language, i.e. Irish or English, and one other language at a level that is appropriate to her/his ability.

3. Creates, appreciates and critically interprets (i.e. questions or analyses) a wide range of texts.

4. Creates and presents artistic works and appreciates the process and skills involved.

5. Has an awareness of personal values and understands the process of moral decision making.

6. Appreciates and respects how diverse values, beliefs and traditions have contributed to the communities and culture in which she/he lives.

7. Values what it means to be an active citizen, with rights and responsibilities on a local and wider scale.

8. Values local, national and international heritage, understands the importance of the relationship between past and current events and the forces that drive change.

9. Understands the origins and impacts of social, economic and environmental aspects of the world around her/him.

10. Has the awareness, knowledge, skills, values and motivation to live sustainably.

11. Takes care of her/his well-being and that of others.

12. Is a confident and competent participant in physical activity and wants to be physically active.

13. Understands the importance of food and diet in making healthy lifestyle choices.

14. Makes informed financial decisions and develops good consumer skills.

15. Recognises the potential uses of mathematical knowledge, skills and understanding in all areas of learning.

16. Describes, illustrates, interprets, predicts and explains patterns and relationships.

17. Comes up with and evaluates strategies for investigating and solving problems using mathematical knowledge, reasoning and skills.

18. Observes and evaluates processes, and asks questions so they can come to valid conclusions.

19. Values the role and contribution of science and technology to society, and their personal, social and global importance.

20. Uses appropriate technologies when faced with a design challenge.

21. Uses practical skills as she/he develops models and products using different materials and technologies.

22. Takes the initiative, is innovative and develops entrepreneurial skills.

23. Brings an idea from its beginnings to achieving its goal.

24. Uses technology and digital media tools to learn, communicate, work and think in co-operation with others, creatively, and in a responsible and ethical way.

Key Skills

A skill can be learned and some skills are considered more important than others; for example, being able to communicate clearly when writing and speaking is probably more important than being able to stand on your head. But both abilities can be learned and developed, which is an important thing to remember about any skill.

We hear a lot today about 'transferable' skills. These are skills or abilities which are not specifically related to any particular job, discipline or task, but are used in a wide variety of work and life situations. Examples include interpersonal skills, critical thinking (being able to objectively analyse and evaluate an issue), etc. These skills are important because they are needed for people to adapt to change and lead meaningful and productive lives.

In the Junior Cycle, these transferable skills or abilities are called Key Skills, which all young people must develop to fully engage with the Senior Cycle and life beyond school. They are not specific to any particular subject, and all subjects must provide learning experiences for young people to develop these skills.

The abilities and qualities developed by young people through these Key Skills are outlined by the NCCA on the following page.

BEING LITERATE

» Developing an understanding and enjoyment of words and language

» Reading for enjoyment and with critical understanding (questioning ideas and issues)

» Writing for different purposes

» Expressing ideas clearly and accurately

» Developing spoken language

» Exploring and creating a variety of texts, including multi-modal texts (e.g. a combination of video and sound on a web page, or pictures and text in a comic)

STAYING WELL

» Being healthy and physically active

» Being social

» Being safe

» Being spiritual

» Being confident

» Being positive about learning

» Being responsible, safe and ethical in using digital technology

MANAGING MYSELF

» Knowing themselves

» Making well-thought-out decisions

» Setting and achieving personal goals

» Being able to reflect on their own learning

» Using digital technology to manage themselves and their learning

MANAGING INFORMATION AND THINKING

» Being curious

» Gathering, recording, organising and evaluating information and data

» Thinking creatively and critically (questioning things)

» Reflecting on and evaluating learning

» Using digital technology to access, manage and share content

BEING NUMERATE

- » Expressing ideas mathematically

- » Estimating, predicting and calculating

- » Developing a positive attitude towards investigating, reasoning and problem-solving

- » Seeing patterns, trends and relationships

- » Gathering, interpreting and representing data

- » Using digital technology to develop numeracy skills and understanding

WORKING WITH OTHERS

- » Developing good relationships and dealing with conflict

- » Co-operating

- » Respecting differences

- » Contributing to making the world a better place

- » Learning with others

- » Working with others through digital technology

BEING CREATIVE

- » Imagining

- » Exploring options and alternatives

- » Putting ideas into practice

- » Learning creatively

- » Stimulating creativity using digital technology

COMMUNICATING

- » Using language

- » Using numbers

- » Listening and expressing themselves

- » Performing and presenting

- » Discussing and debating

- » Using digital technology to communicate

Curriculum

The curriculum is a range of educational programmes within a school. The curriculum for the Junior Cycle comprises:

» **Subjects**

» **Short Courses**

» **Other Learning Experiences**

» **Well-being**

» **Level 2 Learning Programmes**

Subjects

Schools can choose from a total of 21 different subjects on the Junior Cycle programme. These subjects are set down by the Department of Education and the specifications (a detailed description of how things should be done) for each are published by the NCCA.

Each subject has its own specifications. These outline how the subject contributes to the Statements of Learning and the Key Skills, and the learning intentions for that subject, i.e. statements that describe the learning activities/tasks that a lesson or series of lessons will focus on.

A young person can study a maximum of 10 subjects for the Junior Cycle Profile of Achievement (JCPA) certification, or 9 subjects and 2 short courses, or 8 subjects and 4 short courses. All subjects are now studied at a common level, except for English, Irish and Maths, which are still studied at higher and ordinary level.

Short courses

Short courses are a new element of the Junior Cycle programme. They were introduced to allow schools to tailor their learning experiences to the specific needs of their students. Short courses provide a broader range of educational experiences for the Junior Cycle, and also allow schools to recognise and certify different types, and smaller, units of learning.

Short courses can be created 'from scratch' by individual schools – opening up new areas of learning or, alternatively, schools can provide one of the NCCA short courses, which are:

- » Coding
- » Civic, Social and Political Education (CSPE)
- » Physical Education (PE)
- » Digital Media Literacy (DML)
- » A Personal Project: Caring for Animals (Level 2)
- » Social, Personal and Health Education (SPHE)
- » Artistic Performance
- » CSI: Exploring Forensic Science (Level 2)
- » Chinese Language and Culture
- » Philosophy

The short course is designed for approximately 100 hours of student engagement. Most other subjects are designed for 200 hours, except for Irish, English and Maths, which are 240 hours each.

If your child's school offers short courses and you feel these courses suit your child's strengths and interests, they can be of great help and value to them.

Other Areas of Learning

Other Areas of Learning refers to:

1. Co-curricular activities, i.e. activities that tie in with subjects being studied in the school. Examples could include student council, debating, school choir, etc.

2. Extra-curricular activities, i.e. activities that are outside the standard curriculum that students engage in throughout the Junior Cycle. Examples could include sports, charity events, etc.

Students' Other Areas of Learning are recorded in the JCPA, which gives a more balanced and well-rounded view of each student and their success throughout the Junior Cycle. These Other Areas of Learning can also help young people to develop the Key Skills which are so important for success after the Junior Cycle.

Well-being

It is fair to say that all schools have traditionally been doing a lot to support the well-being of their students. However, it is now a dedicated area of study, and is one of the Eight Principles, a Key Skill and an Area of Learning within the Junior Cycle. This emphasis on well-being will make schools' culture, ethos and commitment to well-being more visible and more clearly communicated to students.

All secondary schools must now have 400 hours of timetabled well-being engagement across the three years of the Junior Cycle. These well-being hours will:

» Build on the significant work already taking place in schools in support of students' well-being.

» Include learning opportunities to enhance the physical, mental, emotional and social well-being of students.

Each school develops a programme based on the needs of the students. SPHE, PE, and Career Guidance will all be part of the young person's timetabled well-being hours.

The well-being programmes must enhance, promote and develop the Six Indicators of Student Well-being; these indicators are measures or signals that demonstrate well-being in a young person. They are being:

Active   **Resilient**

Responsible   **Respected/Respectful**

Connected   **Aware**

Below are questions that students, parents and teachers can ask relating to each of the indicators of well-being.

Indicators of Well-being

Active

» Am I a confident and skilled participant in physical activity?

» How physically active am I?

Responsible

» Do I take action to protect and promote my well-being and that of others?

» Do I make healthy eating choices?

» Do I know where my safety is at risk and do I make right choices?

Connected

» Do I feel connected to my school, my friends, my community and the wider world?

» Do I appreciate that my actions and interactions impact on my own well-being and that of others, in local and global contexts?

Resilient

» Do I believe that I have the coping skills to deal with life's challenges?

» Do I know where I can go for help?

» Do I believe that with effort I can achieve?

Respected

» Do I feel that I am listened to and valued?

» Do I have positive relationships with my friends, my peers and my teachers?

» Do I show care and respect for others?

Aware

» Am I aware of my thoughts, feelings and behaviours and can I make sense of them?

» Am I aware of what my personal values are and do I think through my decisions?

» Do I understand what helps me to learn and how I can improve?

All subject teachers are now required to report on how they are supporting the development of student well-being in each of the subjects they teach.

Co- and extra-curricular activities can be a great way for students to develop a sense of being connected to each other, to teachers, and to their school. They give students the opportunity to improve their physical, mental, emotional and social well-being as well as helping them to build key skills, which will be useful to them in work, study or life.

Level 2 Learning Programme

Not all students are ready to follow the full Junior Cycle programme, and the Level 2 Learning Programme (L2LP) was developed to make the curriculum more accessible to students with special educational needs.

Students who undertake an L2LP are those with disabilities categorised as being in the lower mild to higher moderate range of general learning disabilities.

These students will benefit from an L2LP, as it focuses on development and learning in areas like literacy and numeracy, language and communication, mobility and leisure skills (free-time activities), motor coordination, and social and personal development.

Assessment and reporting

Assessment is about gathering information to measure the outcomes of learning. In the old Junior Certificate, this was in the form of a final exam. In the new Junior Cycle, there is a broader use of assessment, and its main purpose is to help and guide the student towards greater learning success. It is used to help learners identify their strengths and any areas of difficulty.

A wide variety of assessment types are used in the Junior Cycle, and they are organised in such a way that the student gets relevant and regular feedback. This means that the teacher will make professional observations and feed them back to the young person on a continual basis.

The emphasis on grades has been greatly reduced. When a teacher is reviewing a piece of work, the objective is not to grade the work, but to give the learner feedback on how the work could be improved. Assessment is now considered most effective when it moves beyond marks and grades, and reporting focuses not just on how the student has done in the past, but on the next steps for further learning.

As a parent, you can expect your child to receive feedback on their learning – it is considered central to building students' ability to manage their own learning, and their motivation to stick with a difficult task or problem.

Although some assessment still involves grading, it should only be seen as one part of a broader approach to assessment. The grading element plays a stronger role as the student approaches the Junior Cycle exams.

As a parent, your child's progress will be reported to you using a new system of reporting that offers a clear picture of your child's learning journey over the three years of the Junior Cycle.

The Classroom-Based Assessment

Classroom-Based Assessments (CBAs) have been introduced as part of the new Junior Cycle to allow students to demonstrate their understanding of skills and concepts that may not be suitable for an externally assessed exam.

Students undertake one CBA per subject in both second year and third year, and these are all assessed at a common level.

The CBA assessments cover a broad range of activities, including oral tasks, written work of different types, practical or designing and making tasks, artistic performances, scientific experiments, projects and other suitable tasks, depending on the subject.

For some subjects (Visual Art, Music, Home Economics and the Technology subjects), the second CBA will involve practical work, the creation of an artefact (a handmade object) or a performance.

CBAs are undertaken by students within class time according to a national timetable, and your child will be given this timetable at the beginning of second year and third year. CBAs will be reported on in the JCPA using the following descriptors:

- » **Exceptional**
- » **Above Expectations**
- » **In Line with Expectations**
- » **Yet to Meet Expectations**

Who grades the CBAs?

The subject department in each school arranges the assessment of the CBAs. To ensure there is consistency across the school, schools organise Subject Learning and Assessment Review (SLAR) meetings with all teachers in the subject department.

Teachers will compare their assessment of students' work and ensure a common approach. Teachers will also have undertaken professional learning to ensure that the CBAs are in line with a national standard, so you can be confident that your child would get a similar descriptor for their CBA from any other teacher in the school or in any other school in the country.

The Assessment Task

During the third year of the Junior Cycle, students complete an Assessment Task in each of their subjects. The Assessment Task is based on the learning outcomes of their second CBA (CBA2).

The Assessment Task is a formal written task, which is set, marked and graded by the State's Examination Division, the SEC (State Examinations Commission), along with the final exam. It is worth 10% of the overall mark for most subjects.

The Assessment Task assesses the young person's:

» ability to evaluate new knowledge or understanding they have gained through their CBA2.

» ability to reflect on the skills they have developed, and to apply them to unfamiliar situations.

State-certified external exam

All Junior Cycle students sit a Junior Cycle written exam in each subject they study, which is set, marked and graded by the SEC.

The written exam is no longer than 2 hours, in a maximum of 10 subjects. All subjects are common level except for English, Irish and Maths, which have both higher and ordinary levels.

The exams are held in June of third year for all subjects, and they are part of a comprehensive range of assessments that make up the Junior Cycle Profile of Achievement (JCPA).

The new grading system

If you have been through the Irish education system, you are probably familiar with the old grading system A, B, C, D, E, F and NG. This system has been replaced by the following descriptors:

Distinction	90 to 100%
Higher Merit	75 to 89%
Merit	55 to 74%
Achieved	40 to 54%
Partially Achieved	20 to 39%
Not graded	0 to 19%

You may be wondering at this stage: what is staying the same? Well, here are some of the things that will remain the same:

» Students will continue to experience a broad and balanced curriculum.

» Standards and expectations remain high.

» The Department of Education and Skills will monitor quality across all schools.

» The State Examination Commission will continue to be involved in assessment for certification.

Moreover, as a result of the Junior Cycle, the following areas are improving:

» A better and more engaging learning experience for your child

» Updated subject specifications

» Quality reporting back to parents and students

» Assessment to support learning

» An emphasis on Key Skills and preparation for life

The Junior Cycle Profile of Achievement

The Junior Cycle Profile of Achievement (JCPA) is the award your child will receive at the end of their Junior Cycle. It will actually be issued by the school during the first term of transition year/fifth year.

The JCPA outlines the achievements of the young person across the range of their learning during the Junior Cycle. It will cover State Examination results, Classroom-Based Assessment results and Other Areas of Learning. It includes:

» The results from the written exams in June in each subject.

» The descriptors for each of the CBAs.

» A description of Other Areas of Learning undertaken or achieved by the student.

JUNIOR CYCLE PROFILE OF ACHIEVEMENT

2017

John Kelly

DOB: 21 June 2001

STATE CERTIFIED FINAL EXAMINATIONS

Examination number: 456985

English (O)	Distinction
Irish (O) (2)	A
Mathematics (H)	B
History (H)	C
Geography (H)	D
French (O) (2)	C
Business Studies (H)	B
Science (H)	B
C.S.P.E. (C)	A

Classroom-Based Assessments - English

Oral Communication	Above expectations
Collection of Texts	In line with expectations

Classroom-Based Assessments - Short Courses

Coding	In line with expectations
Physical Education	Above expectations
Artistic Performance	Exceptional
Philosophy	In line with expectations

SAMPLE

Other Areas of Learning

The school has flexibility to report on other learning experiences/events that the student has participated in outside the formal timetabled curriculum such as;

- Engagement with co-curricular or extra-curricular activities such as a science fair, school's sporting activities or debating.

- Specific learning opportunities that do not form part of subjects or short courses, i.e; leadership training; activities relating to guidance; membership of school clubs or societies; membership of school's student council.

- Engagements that form part of the formal timetabled curriculum but not reported on in other sections of the JCPA i.e; engagement with a school's own religious education programme or with elements of the PE, SPHE curriculum and CSPE.

Principal	**Year Head**	**Roll Number:** 600900
Ms Mary Ryan	MR. Jack Quigley	Anytown Secondary School Anytown, Co. Anytown V94 HXW5

Anytown Secondary School

This JCPA recognises and records achievements in Junior Cycle.

Supporting your child throughout the Junior Cycle

Supporting your child throughout the Junior Cycle

As you can see from the previous section, there is quite a lot involved in the new Junior Cycle. The key role you played in supporting and encouraging your child in their transition into secondary school continues throughout the Junior Cycle. Some of the simple support strategies you read about earlier continue to apply, and here are a few more to go along with them.

Having conversations about learning

As your child matures, your role as a parent also changes. Your child will be developing greater independence and you will be very much a coach, guide and sounding board for them.

The key to supporting any teenager is to show interest rather than interfere. If a teenager feels you are intruding into their space/life, they can shut you out, or even begin to rebel. This can be a difficult path to manage, but here are some simple tips that may help.

In short, try to learn to listen and to support your child, have mature conversations with them, and give fewer instructions.

TIPS ON BEING A GOOD LISTENER

One of the biggest complaints of young people is that they are not listened to by their parents, teachers or other significant adults. This is why they more often than not turn to their peers for advice or reassurance. Listening is a skill, and it takes practice.

ACTIVE LISTENING

Active listening is understanding what someone is saying, without judgement or expectation. In a conversation, it involves concentrating, understanding, responding and remembering what is being said.

The following are some helpful **"SHUSH"** listening tips:

SHOW YOU CARE

» Focus on the other person.

» Make eye contact.

» Put away your phone.

» When starting the conversation, don't talk about yourself.

» Aim to learn at least one new thing about the person who is talking to you.

HAVE PATIENCE

It may take time and several attempts before your child will be ready to talk, so don't put them under pressure to open up. If they pause during their response, wait; they may not have finished speaking. Remember:

» It might take some time for them to think about what they're saying.

» They may find it difficult to explain how they are feeling.

» Effective listening is about trusting the other person. They trust you to listen and not to judge.

Through non-judgemental listening, you are allowing your child to relax into the conversation. They can use it as a place to reflect or work through difficult emotions.

USE OPEN QUESTIONS

Ask open-ended questions that will make your child pause, think, reflect and expand. They often start with 'how' or 'what'. For example, asking, "How do you feel about your situation?" This can open up a conversation more than saying something like, "Do you feel depressed?"

The hope is that the open-ended questions will bring whatever is bothering them out in the open to figure it out. Another good question is to ask, "Can you tell me a bit more about that?" Avoid asking closed questions, or saying something that closes down the conversation. Open-ended questions encourage someone to talk.

SAY IT BACK

Check you've understood, but don't interrupt or offer a solution. Repeating something back to somebody is a good way to let someone know you are paying attention. You can check to see that you're hearing what they want you to hear.

HAVE COURAGE

Don't be put off by a negative response and don't feel you have to fill a silence. It can feel intrusive to ask someone how they feel. You'll soon see if someone is uncomfortable and doesn't want to engage with you at that level. Sometimes it's exactly what somebody needs – to be able to share what's going on in their mind.

Talking to your child about their learning experiences

As parents, we tend to ask quite general questions, like, 'How was your day?' But we are more likely to generate a conversation if we ask more specific questions, like:

» How are you coping in maths class?

» What subject do you like most?

» How did you cope with any difficulties and/or did you ask for help?

These questions will encourage your child to reflect on their learning – this is a huge part of the Junior Cycle in terms of making learning more meaningful for students.

Encouraging and supporting your child's learning

Throughout the Junior Cycle, your child will be engaged in:

» Reviewing feedback from their teachers and identifying what they have done well

» Identifying what they should do next

» Setting and achieving personal targets

» Drafting and redrafting and correcting their own work

» Giving feedback to their peers

» Looking at examples of good work and identifying how they can improve on their own work.

Ask your child to share their feedback with you – encourage them to set and achieve learning targets. The key is that they focus on their strengths and work on their weak points. Too often, we limit ourselves by only seeing our weaknesses. By focusing on your child's strength, you are building their confidence, highlighting what they can do, rather than what they can't.

Supporting your child - Preparing for Classroom-Based Assessments (CBAs)

Talk to your child about their CBAs. If the CBA is a presentation, you might get them to practise it in front of you. When doing this, you can support them by asking questions and offering advice/feedback. You could also ask them what feedback they have received so far, and open a conversation with them around applying that feedback.

It is important to remember, however, that the CBAs are low stakes, i.e. they are designed to support learning rather than assess your child's progress in learning. They should be similar to normal class time. If the child is anxious, discuss the source of the anxiety and consider discussing the issues with the class teacher.

Forming good study habits

As you know, if material is not reviewed it will be forgotten, and it's important that your child develops a study system.

As a parent, your key task is to highlight to your child the importance of study as preparation for exams. Exams do not measure ability, they measure knowledge – and your child can gain this knowledge through focused study.

Learning to Learn is now one of the key principles of the Junior Cycle, and young people in Junior Cycle will be shown how to study for their different subjects. During the early years in secondary school, and if your child is open to it, you could use the tried and tested method of examining your child. You hold the book, list, card etc. and gently examine the child on the material they have revised.

This method can help strengthen the parent-child bond, because it shows that you are willing to help take on the burden of study.

As a parent, you should try to ensure that your child has a suitable place to work, and that they also have a structure around their week, so that they have a time to study each day, particularly in the exam year.

Preparing for parent-teacher meetings

Most schools arrange an annual parent-teacher meeting/evening for each year group in their school. While different schools organise these meetings in different ways, the most common arrangement is still for parents to meet each of their child's teachers for approximately 5 minutes.

Another method that's becoming popular is for the parents to meet the form teacher, who will communicate the overall progress of their child across all subjects.

Schools arrange parent-teacher meetings because they know that you are your child's first teacher. Your child's teachers will learn about your child's needs from you, and no doubt you will also learn about your child's learning strengths and the supports needed from their teachers. When parents and teachers work in partnership, the winner is the child. So, below are tips to make the most of parent-teacher meetings.

The main focus of the meeting will be how your child is getting on in school and to talk about how they might further improve. The emphasis in the Junior Cycle is around the development of Key Skills (See Section II), so you can expect your child's teachers to refer to the development of these Key Skills as well as the progress they are making within their subject areas.

You can prepare for the parent-teacher meeting by talking to your child about school and their progress, both academically and their development of the Key Skills. You might have a conversation with your child to find out:

» **The subjects/short courses and Other Areas of Learning that they are undertaking. Try to get an understanding of any challenges that your child is experiencing with different subjects.**

» **The teachers' names: The school may supply you with a list of your child's teachers; if not, ask your child to give you a list of their teachers by subject.**

» How they feel about school

» How they feel about each subject/short course or Other Area of Learning

» What they consider to be their learning strengths

» How they feel their development of Key Skills is progressing

» How they feel about their well-being, mental health and ability to deal with the everyday stresses of school life

» If there is anything they'd like you to talk to their teacher about

» Give your child the space to talk to you about anything that may be affecting them in school.

» Review previous reports: Remind yourself of your child's performance and their teachers' comments in previous reports. Be ready to ask the teachers for any updates since these reports.

Preparing for the meeting

Having spoken to your child, you might now create a list of questions to ask different subject teachers. Obviously, no two parents will ask the same questions, but some typical questions might include:

» Is my child's progress in line with their ability?

» Does my child complete assignments and homework to a high standard and on time?

» Do they seem to be fully engaged in the learning?

» Are they co-operative and respectful to teachers and other students?

» Do they seem to have a good range of friends?

» What can I do to help them achieve their learning potential?

» Are there additional learning supports that my child can get in school?

In some cases, you may receive feedback from the teacher that you weren't expecting. If they require further engagement from you, try to agree a plan of action with them. This can be done during the parent-teacher meeting or at a follow-up meeting.

The plan would really be an agreement on how both you and the teacher support your child. You should record what you will do, when you will do it, and how often. If necessary, make plans to communicate with the teacher on a more regular basis.

Remember that the parent-teacher meeting is about your child, so it's important to have a conversation about it with your child soon after the meeting. Share with them what you learned, and emphasise the positive. If you are going to further support your child's learning at home as a result of the parent-teacher meeting, let your child know what this support will look like. Always include them in the decision-making as much as possible. Give them choices so that they can be as much in charge of their own learning as possible, but let them know that you are there to support them on their learning journey.

You receive a Note of Concern from the school...

Schools expect parents to be more involved than ever in supporting their child's learning. As a parent, therefore, you might receive a Note of Concern from your child's teacher or school about their behaviour, performance or attendance. What do you do?

While no parent wants to receive these notes, it's not the end of the world, and the first thing to do if you do get a note is to remain calm. It is of course worrying to hear that your child may be misbehaving or under-performing in school, and it's natural to have concerns about that.

All young people go through ups and downs on their learning journey, so whatever is going on is most likely to be a part of growing up.

As a parent, it's important that you listen to your child, try to establish the facts, but also remain supportive of the school. Teaching is a challenging job at the best of times, so teachers need parents' support.

You should try to understand what is happening in school, to get to the bottom of why it is happening, and to find out if your child needs additional support from you or from other professionals.

If your child is misbehaving, ask them why. Is it related to particular subjects? Other students? Situations? While you are trying to get to the truth, be aware that you may not be hearing the full story.

If the Note of Concern is about dropping grades, try to find out why, and to come up with a plan to help your child to achieve their potential.

If there is a serious issue, it's worth meeting your child's teacher and putting a plan in place to support your child. One of the main reasons young people fall behind is that there is a lack of structure in relation to homework and study. We have shared tips about establishing this structure in your house (see pages 19-24).

As a parent supporting the school, schoolwork and homework should be prioritised, and a time should be allocated each day for your child to complete this work.

You may also need to get more actively involved in supporting your child by reviewing their homework, and helping them with study. This can be time-consuming, but some children do need this additional support in the early years of the Junior Cycle. Sometimes you'll need to have a frank conversation with your child:

"Until your grades improve, I'm going to set up a study time. I will supervise it and there will be no phone or internet. When your grades improve, I'll allow you take more control over your own learning/study routine again."

You should, of course, show an interest in what your child is doing in school, ask them questions, etc.

IF YOU RECEIVE A NOTE OF CONCERN, YOU SHOULD:

» Remain calm

» Determine the facts

» Listen to your child

» Talk to your child's teacher if necessary

» Support the school

» Devise a plan that helps your child improve their behaviour/performance, etc.

Building relationships with the school

When parents and teachers have strong relationships, there are benefits for the child. So, as a parent, you should, whenever possible, attend parent-teacher meetings and school public meetings, or volunteer to support fundraising events. If you have time, you might join the parents' council – this would give you a better insight into the school. You would also become more familiar with the language of the school, and thus be better able to support your child.

Not all parents can be involved in the school as much as they'd like, but you can still let your child know that school is important to your family. Talking about school with your child, being warm and friendly at school events, and being positive about the school and its staff, sends the message that you value education and are interested in what's happening for your child at school.

Post-primary schools are complex organisations, and it's challenging to develop a relationship with all of your child's teachers. However, it's worth knowing in particular your child's form teacher/tutor and year head, for them to know that you see the education of your child as a partnership, and that you want to play a supporting role.

Bullying

Bullying is the ongoing abuse of another person, either physically or mentally. The humiliation felt by the victim can be terrible, and if it occurs over a long period of time it can have devastating effects on mental health.

Types of bullying

» Physical bullying involves harmful actions against another person's body, such as hitting, pinching or kicking. It might also involve interfering with another person's property. Some examples include stealing or damaging things.

» Verbal bullying is talking to a person, or about a person, in a way that is unkind and hurtful, for example, teasing, name-calling, spreading rumours or whispering.

» Non-verbal bullying refers to all the behaviour that upsets, excludes or embarrasses another person, for example, leaving someone out of a game or activity on purpose, making rude gestures at someone or writing hate notes about a person that will upset them.

As a parent, you should ensure that your child knows that if someone is deliberately and repeatedly doing or saying things to them that they find hurtful, upsetting, annoying, worrying, frustrating, embarrassing or humiliating, they are being bullied. If they are being bullied in school, or if someone they know is being bullied, please encourage them to take the first step of telling a teacher or asking a parent or a school friend to do so for them.

If you are concerned about a change in your child's general mood or behaviour, it may not be "just hormones." Your child may be experiencing bullying. To put your mind at ease, please contact the school and make teachers aware of your concerns. They can then investigate, and if there is bullying taking place, they can bring the bullying to an end without making matters worse for your child or anyone else.

Even little negative things, which would be only slightly upsetting if they happened just once, can be very hurtful when repeated over and over again. While bullying behaviour is hurtful, those deliberately doing it usually do not understand or intend the level of damage it can cause. Bullying is very secretive, but there may be clues that indicate that it is happening.

WHAT CAN YOU DO IF YOU SUSPECT THAT YOUR CHILD IS BEING BULLIED?

» Don't be angry. Being angry can make matters worse and usually does not help resolve the problem. Talk to your child calmly.

» Reassure your child that the problem lies with the bully, not them.

» Try to find out what's happening, but don't be surprised if your child doesn't want to tell you – don't try to force the issue, but offer to help find a "win-win" resolution to end the bullying.

» Notify the school of your concerns and ask for help. Schools can now effectively investigate and resolve bullying situations.

» Cyberbullying can be traceable after the event, but by then, damage may have been done, so parents should proactively monitor their children's use of electronic media (e.g. phones) and social media, and ensure that precautions have been taken to minimise the risk of cyberbullying.

Schools' obligations in relation to bullying

The Department of Education and Skills issued new Anti-Bullying Procedures to all schools in 2013, which schools are required to follow. These procedures require schools to have a consistent and clear approach to investigating and dealing with bullying when it happens, to establish intervention strategies to minimise it, and to ensure that bullying behaviour is always recorded, investigated and followed-up.

Through an awareness-raising programme, the Department of Education wants pupils to be better informed about how hurtful and unacceptable bullying behaviour is, as pupils who recognise bullying behaviour are less likely to bully others and more likely to report it when they see it. It wants:

1. Bullying situations to be "resolved", achieving a "win-win" outcome, and

2. Relationships to be "restored" to the level before the bullying began. This should be done while at the same time avoiding blame and punishment, as it has been shown that these do not work.

> A free website that supports schools in this approach can be found at
> *www.antibullyingcampaign.ie*

Online safety for your child

Cyberbullying is another way your child can be bullied. For useful information on internet safety, see *www.webwise.ie*.

Webwise is the Irish Internet Safety Awareness Centre. It is co-funded by the Department of Education and Skills and co-financed by the European Union's Connecting Europe Facility. Webwise promotes the safer use of the internet through sharing information with parents, teachers, and children themselves.

At *www.webwise.ie*, you will find lots of advice to support your child's online life. They also have a range of youth-orientated resources, which you should encourage your child to read.

TOP TIPS TO PROTECT YOUR CHILD FROM CYBERBULLYING BY MOBILE PHONE

Make sure:

» Their phone is password protected and that they don't give the password to anyone except you.

» They only give their phone number to people they trust.

» They never send pictures of themselves or others, or personal messages, by phone to anyone who cannot be totally trusted not to pass them on to someone else.

» That if someone gets their number and starts making unwelcome calls or sending unwelcome messages or pictures to them, no matter how annoyed or upset they are, they should not reply. They should not delete the pictures or messages, and should not remove a record of the calls from their phone's log. Instead, they should tell a parent, a teacher or other adult they trust.

Additional and Special Educational Needs (SEN)

No two children are the same, and no two children learn at the same pace. If you believe that your child needs additional educational supports at school, you should contact their subject teacher/class tutor/year head/guidance counsellor/special education team to discuss your concerns.

When talking to an educational professional, it helps if you are specific about the exact nature of your concerns and how long you have had them.

What are Additional or Special Educational Needs?

These are difficulties experienced by students that make it harder for them to achieve success as easily as their peers. These students need extra support to enable them to reach their true potential. Challenges include (but are not limited to):

» Specific learning difficulties, e.g. dyslexia, dyscalculia

» General learning difficulties (mild/borderline mild/moderate)

» Speech and language difficulties

» Physical difficulties, e.g. cerebral palsy, Developmental Co-ordination Disorder (DCD/Dyspraxia)

» Visual or hearing impairment

» Autistic Spectrum Disorder (ASD)/Asperger's

» Down's Syndrome

» Attention Deficit (Hyperactive)Disorder (ADD/ADHD)

» Emotional disturbance/anxiety disorders

» Behavioural disorders

» Medical/health issues

Information about these difficulties is available on the Special Education Support Service website *www.sess.ie*

How are SEN departments resourced?

The Department of Education and Science (DES) supplies the Special Education Teaching hours allocation, SNA support, IT and other specialised equipment for students with SEN. SEN hours/allocation are decided in relation to the needs and profile of the school as a whole. Applications are made to the Special Educational Needs Officer (SENO) for SNA support and IT equipment, and these are guided by students' psychological and/or occupational therapy reports.

The SENO's decision is communicated to the school and DES. The DES will then approve the SNA/IT support, enabling the school, with parental/guardian consent, to put the appropriate supports in place.

The SEN department normally works closely with the guidance department, chaplaincy and year heads, as well as SNAs, parents and outside agencies, to support students with additional or special educational needs.

In-school support

Typically, students with special educational needs are supported educationally in a variety of ways, depending on their needs and the resources available. This includes:

- » Learning support for literacy/numeracy classes

- » One-to-one or small group resource classes as appropriate, for those with very specific needs

- » Team-teaching in mainstream classes, to maximise support and subject choice

- » A modified or reduced curriculum, as recommended or necessary

- » Exemptions from Irish, in line with current DES guidelines

- » Special Needs Assistants (SNAs), in line with current guidelines

- » IT or other equipment, as appropriate

- » Reasonable Accommodations in the State certified exams.

If your child has special educational needs, both you and your child should be consulted and involved in the decisions relating to the best supports for them.

How are students with SEN identified?

Schools have a variety of ways to identify students with SEN, these include:

- » Entrance assessment tests
- » National school feedback
- » Parental concerns/feedback
- » Psychological/occupational therapy/other assessment and reports
- » Teacher referrals
- » In-school standardised testing
- » Monitoring of ongoing school performance (school tests and reports)
- » Student self-referral to the SEN department.

Special Education Teaching Allocation

There is a Special Education Teaching Allocation that allows each school to provide additional teaching support for all pupils who need it, based on their individual learning needs.

The Department has set out what is known as the 'Continuum of Support' framework to help schools to identify and respond to students' needs. This framework recognises that special educational needs can range from mild to severe, and from short- to long-term, and that students need different levels of support depending on their identified educational needs.

Using this framework helps to ensure that interventions move from class-based to more intensive and individualised support, and that they are guided by careful monitoring of progress.

Continuum of Support

Using the Continuum of Support framework, schools can identify students' educational needs - including academic, social and emotional needs - as well as needs associated with physical, sensory, language and communication difficulties.

Many students will have had their special educational needs identified before starting secondary school. It is important for schools to obtain information on students' learning from primary schools and parents, in order to ensure continuity and progression in the student's education.

The National Council for Curriculum and Assessment (NCCA) has developed materials to support the reporting and transfer of pupil information from primary to post-primary schools.

These include:

» **6th class report card**

» **My Profile sheet for children**

» **My Child's Profile sheet for parent(s)**

A ***Special Educational Needs Summary Form*** is included to support the sharing of information for children with identified learning needs.

Primary schools are required to use the 'Education Passport' materials listed above, and to send them to the relevant secondary school once enrolment is confirmed, ideally by the end of June.

> For more information, see
> ***www.sess.ie/resources/transition-primary-post-primary***

For students with a high level of need, meetings are sometimes arranged between primary and secondary schools before the school year starts.

The Post-Primary Transfer Review Form is a useful template for gathering information on students' academic and personal development needs. This information is then used to plan any intervention needed in the new school.

Your child's school may use its own assessment practices to support the planning process for your child if they have SEN. Resources such as the Drumcondra Online Testing System can be used for this purpose. Depending on your child's needs, learning supports can be offered in different ways as shown below:

» Whole-school and Classroom Support for All – a preventative and proactive approach

» School Support for Some – a response to groups and individuals

» School Support Plus (support for a few) – individualised and specialist support

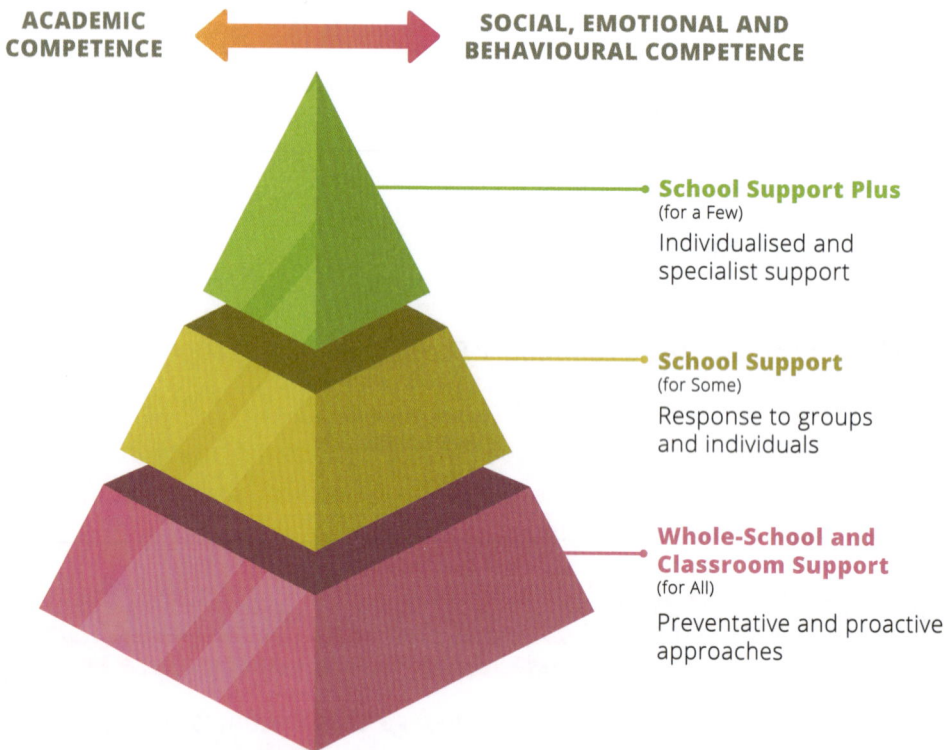

ACADEMIC COMPETENCE

SOCIAL, EMOTIONAL AND BEHAVIOURAL COMPETENCE

School Support Plus
(for a Few)
Individualised and specialist support

School Support
(for Some)
Response to groups and individuals

Whole-School and Classroom Support
(for All)
Preventative and proactive approaches

A Continuum of Support

Special education teaching supports provided to schools should only be used to support pupils with identified special educational needs, including pupils for whom English is an Additional Language (EAL); they should not be used to reduce the pupil-teacher ratio in mainstream classes.

The SEN resource teaching model promotes a strong, inclusive culture with a focus on aiming high and improving outcomes for all students. This involves collaborative action by the school community to improve student learning, behaviour and well-being.

Multiple intelligences

One of the best ways you can support your child is to understand that each young person is unique, with their own strengths, talents and abilities. If you can help them to identify their key strengths, and encourage them to develop and build on them, it will be a huge support to give them.

There was a time when we had a very narrow definition of intelligence, and thought young people were intelligent if they were good academically. Today, however, the question is not whether your child is intelligent, but what their main strengths or intelligences are.

We now have a much better understanding of intelligence and ability, thanks to the work of Howard Gardner, a Harvard professor who developed the theory of multiple intelligences.

Gardner showed that we don't just have 'an' intelligence - we have at least eight of them, and our natural ability in each of them is different.

Howard Gardner's eight intelligences are:

LINGUISTIC
good at using words, both written and spoken; enjoys writing stories, reading, etc.

MATHEMATICAL
good at reasoning, analysing and solving problems.

KINAESTHETIC
good at body movement, sport, dance, hand-eye co-ordination and dexterity.

SPATIAL
good at visualising things, at reading maps, charts, drawing, etc.

MUSICAL
good with rhythms and sounds, musical composition and performances; a good appreciation for music.

INTERPERSONAL
can understand and relate well to other people; good at understanding the emotions and needs of others.

INTRAPERSONAL
good at interpersonal reflection and analysis; tends to have very high self-awareness.

NATURALISTIC
in tune with nature and interested in nurturing and protecting the environment.

Normally, people are stronger in three or four of these intelligences; these can be called a person's strengths. Young people tend to do best when they build on their strengths, so if you can help them to identify these strengths and encourage them to develop them you will certainly be helping to maximise their potential.

Fixed versus growth mindset

Based on Howard Gardner's multiple intelligences theory, each of us have natural strengths, and so some things come easier to us. What is also true, though, is that most abilities can be developed with persistence and practice. It's important that young people realise their abilities are not fixed, but rather can grow.

Carol Dweck is a Stanford professor whose research challenges the belief that intelligent people are born smart, and she has shown that a person's mindset has a big impact on their performance. She has identified two types of mindset:

The fixed mindset

Sometimes, if young people are not good at maths or learning languages, or a certain sport, they might say, 'I'm just not built to do this', or 'My brain is not wired to be good at that!'

They may also think that, no matter how much effort they put in, they will never be good at it. This is what Carol Dweck called a 'fixed mindset'. People with a fixed mindset believe that their ability or intelligence for a particular thing is fixed – hardwired, as it were – and there is nothing they can do to increase their ability in that area.

People with a fixed mindset tend to give up on things if they fail the first time; they see no point in practising, as they feel that their ability to do something will never change. Most of us have felt like this at one time or another, especially when it comes to school subjects, which might be part of the reason students end up having some subjects they don't like and some they really enjoy! A fixed mindset can limit a young person's desire to stick with something, and so limits their chances of success.

The growth mindset

The good news is there's another way we can view our intelligence or abilities – what Carol Dweck called the 'growth mindset'. With a growth mindset, we believe that if we keep practising something, our intelligence or ability for that activity can grow, is adaptable and can improve.

Unlike a fixed mindset, students with a growth mindset don't give up when they fail at something the first time; instead they see struggle as a natural part of the process of learning something, and also see feedback from teachers and others as an opportunity to identify how they can improve.

People with a growth mindset tend to be more resilient when it comes to learning, in the sense that they stick at something until they eventually get good at it.

The growth mindset theory is strongly supported by recent studies in neuroscience: we now know that the physical structure of the brain grows and changes with repeated and directed attention towards any behaviour, whether it's learning, physical activity, emotions or any other cognitive activity.

Choosing your mindset

So, the good news is that if we do something over and over again, like practise or study, we actually create new pathways in the brain for doing that activity and eventually become good at it. You've heard the saying, 'practice makes perfect'; well, we like to think of this as 'practice makes permanent'!

In simple terms, mindset is a choice. And it's important that young people choose to have a growth mindset; it's just a matter of understanding that their ability to do anything grows with practice. With patience, their brain will adapt and they will become good at doing the task!

One of the greatest gifts you can give your child is to help them discover their own strengths, to encourage them to build on those strengths, while also giving them the confidence to understand that, with practice, they can develop their capability in any area.

This growth mindset will help them excel in school, and also prepare them for the challenges of life ahead. They will keep learning and growing their intelligence, and with practice, grow to become well-rounded, adaptable young people, bringing their valuable skill sets into life and work beyond school.

Appendices

Appendix 1: Useful contacts

Aware	Helping defeat depression	1890 303302 www.aware.ie
Belong to	Supports lesbian, gay, bisexual and trans young people in Ireland	(01) 670 6223 www.belongto.org
Bodywhys	The Eating Disorders Association of Ireland	1890 200 444 www.bodywhys.ie
Childline	Confidential helpline for children and young people	1800 66 66 66 Text 50101 www.childline.ie
Children First	National Guidelines for the Protection and Welfare of Children	www.tusla.ie/children-first
Common Sense Media	Expert reviews and objective advice for parents about online resources	www.commonsensemedia.org
Connect Safety	Educates users of connected technology about safety, privacy and security	www.connectsafety.org
ISPCC	The Irish Society for the Prevention of Cruelty to Children is Ireland's national child protection charity	01 6767960 www.ispcc.ie

National Anti-Bullying Centre (ABC)	Provides schools with tools to deal effectively with bullying.	www.antibullyingcampaign.ie
The National Council for Curriculum and Assessment	Works with learners, teachers, parents and practitioners to develop research-based curriculum and assessment	www.ncca.ie
National LGBT Helpline	The National LGBT Helpline provides a support service for lesbian, gay, bisexual and transgender people.	1890 929 539 www.lgbt.ie
Pieta House	Centre for prevention of self-harm and suicide.	01 601 0000 www.pieta.ie
Samaritans Helpline	The Samaritans offer confidential, non-judgemental support 24 hours a day.	1850 6060 90 jo@samaritans.org www.samaritans.org
Shine	Supporting people affected by mental health.	1890 621 631 www.shineonline.ie
St. Patrick's Mental Health Services	Provides mental health services to teenagers and adults.	(01) 249 3200 www.walkinmyshoes.ie
SpunOut	SpunOut.ie is Ireland's youth information website created by young people, for young people.	Text SPUNOUT to 086 1800 280. Standard SMS rates may apply www.spunout.ie
Webwise	Offers free information, advice and resources to help parents, teachers and students address internet safety issues.	internetsafety@pdst.ie www.webwise.ie

Appendix 2: Educational terms explained

Assessment Task	A written task completed by students during third year during class time and sent to the SEC for marking.
Classroom-Based Assessment (CBA)	This involves the teacher assessing the student on a particular task that they have prepared during class time over a defined time period.
Classroom-Based Assessment Grade Descriptors	When a student has completed their CBAs, their teacher awards them a Grade Descriptor. The descriptors are: Exceptional, Above Expectations, In Line with Expectations, Yet to Meet Expectations.
Curriculum	This refers to the programmes of study offered by a school. For the Junior Cycle, the curriculum is a combination of subjects, short courses and other areas of learning.
Co-Curricular Activities	These are activities and learning experiences that complement what is being taught in class; for example, participating in the BT Young Scientist project, or activities that support Science, English, Maths, etc.
Extra-Curricular Activities	These are activities outside the standard curriculum that students engage in throughout their Junior Cycle; for example, sports, fundraising, etc.

Formative Assessment	This does not form part of a student's final grade, but provides constructive feedback to the learner, with a view to improving learning and understanding.
Junior Cycle Profile of Achievement (JCPA)	This is the certificate students get at the end of third year, showing their SEC exam results, CBAs for subjects and short courses, and Other Areas of Learning.
Key Skills	These are the transferable skills which young people are expected to develop during the Junior Cycle. The eight Key Skills are: Staying well; Working with others; Managing information and thinking; Managing myself; Communicating; Being literate; Being creative; Being numerate.
Statements of Learning	24 Statements that cover the broad spectrum of what students are expected to know by the end of the Junior Cycle. Each subject covers some of the statements.
Subject Specification	A document outlining the content, structure and principles of learning to take place in each subject.
Summative Assessment	Evaluates students' learning at the end of a period of learning. It looks back on past learning and the performance of students. It is usually marked, and compared with previous assessments. Its purpose is to determine to what degree students have demonstrated understanding of their learning.

Appendix 3: Acronyms and Abbreviations used in Education

CSPE	Civic, Social and Political Education
DEIS	Delivering Equality of Opportunity in Schools
DES	Department of Education and Skills
ETB	Education and Training Board
ICT	Information and Communication Technology
IEP	Individual Education Plan
JC	Junior Cycle
LC	Leaving Certificate
LCA	Leaving Certificate Applied Programme
LCVP	Leaving Certificate Vocational Programme
NCCA	National Council for Curriculum and Assessment
NEPS	National Educational Psychological Service
PTR	Pupil Teacher Ratio
SEC	State Examinations Commission
SLSS	Second Level Support Service
SPHE	Social, Personal and Health Education
TY	Transition Year

Appendix 4: Abbreviations used in Special Education

ADHD	Attention Deficit Hyperactive Disorder
AHEAD	Association for Higher Education Access and Disability
ASD	Autistic Spectrum Disorder
DARE	Disability Access Route to Education
DCD	Developmental Coordination Disorder
EBD	Emotional Behavioural Disorder
HEAR	Higher Education Access Route
MGLD	Mild General Learning Difficulties
NCSE	National Council for Special Education
NCTE	National Council for Technology in Education
NDA	National Disability Authority
NEWB	National Education Welfare Board
ODD	Oppositional Defiant Disorder
RACE	Reasonable Accommodations for Certificate Exams
SEN	Special Educational Needs
SENO	Special Educational Needs Officer
SLD	Specific Learning Difficulty
SNA	Special Needs Assistant